Table of Contents

Introduction

Many people would love to sew, but they do not go beyond giving a few stitches with the needle and thread. However, everything changes when you have a sewing machine, because many jobs can be done in a very short time. For this, learning to sew by machine is essential, something for which you have to have a little patience.

If you are here it is because you have already decided to **learn how to machine sew**!! Congratulations!! Now you can start creating your own designs and give free rein to your imagination. However, before starting to take your first steps in the sewing area, you should know some basic notions. Remember that everything you have learned must be practiced so that you can achieve success in a short time.
In the next topics I will show you all the aspects you must know so that you learn to sew by machine. It does not matter if your experience on the subject is at zero, the important thing is to **take that first step** and you are here!

Why should you learn to machine sew?

There are those who have a sewing machine at home and do not know how to use it or do not dare to touch it. Others have always wanted to **buy a sewing machine** and want to learn how to use it. But, there are those who do very well with hand sewing, and are missing out on all the advantages of machine sewing.

In any case, it will always be a point to have the virtue of **knowing how to sew on a machine**. Below I will give you some reasons that will convince you to enter this magical and useful world of sewing.

Now if you don't already have a sewing machine then the first step is to help you choose one. If you are looking for a cheap sewing machine, this guide is going to help you with that. If on the contrary you are looking to become an expert and want an all-terrain sewing machine then our guide on the best professional sewing machines is what you are looking for.

You will save time

When you do well by hand sewing, you will undoubtedly do better by machine sewing. One of the most attractive aspects of sewing with a machine is **the speed** with which you can finish a project. Remember that **time is life!**

You can sew for yourself

Machine sewing will not only allow you to work on your own, but you can also make **your own outfits**. As your experience grows, machine sewing will become easier and faster. Once you take a liking to it, there is no going back.

You give more

If you have a sewing machine to carry out your sewing projects, you will finish on time to **attend to new projects**. The more work you have, the more experience and skill you will grow. The important thing is not the amount of work you carry out, but rather that each project carried out be better and more beautiful. Your clients will love your jobs!

Parts of the Sewing Machine

A sewing machine has a large number of elements:

Machine roulette is the name given to a wheel on one side. By turning it, it allows us to puncture or remove the needle from the fabric. It is very useful when the needle gets stuck. Also, instead of using the machine pedal, you can start small by turning this wheel. It will go much slower, but it helps to learn little by little.

The reverse lever is a small device that many modern sewing machines have. It can be said that it is the button for reversing, making it ideal for seam finishing.

At the top of the machine, we find the bobbin holders, where the thread goes. Depending on the thickness of the thread, we can adjust a small thread. As a general rule, they can be selected from 0 to 9, always depending on the thickness of the fabrics.

Within the large number of buttons that we can find on a sewing machine, we find those of choosing the width and length of the stitch. In each of them, you have to select the right number, depending on what you need. If we choose 0, we will make several stitches in the same place. The 1 is a very short stitch, suitable for buttonholes. The number 2 is for normal stitching and older serve to baste stitches.

Electric sewing machines have a small drawer that can be removed. Here is the metal bobbin holder, easy to remove. We will only have to slide a front tab. Inside is the bobbin with its corresponding thread.

The seam plate is the base where both the presser foot and the needle rests and is where what are known as drive teeth are located.

The presser foot can be raised or lowered thanks to a lever on the back of the machine. To be able to thread the needle, the presser foot must be raised.

Although there are many machine models, most of its most outstanding functions are standardized in each of its models. Know what they are:

Graduation wheel

It corresponds to the wheel located on the side of the machine. This wheel is rotated and allows you to puncture or remove the needle from the fabric. It is usually very useful when the needle is stuck, and must be removed manually.

Sometimes you could use the roulette to **start working** the machine, instead of using the pedal. This process is considered much slower, but it is certainly safer.

Stitch selection buttons

These buttons allow you to **adjust the width and length** of the stitch. For this you must select the number according to your needs. If you want to reinforce the stitch you can use Zero (0), with this number you will make several stitches in one place. However, if you want to make short stitches use number 1, for example a buttonhole. For its part, number 2 is considered normal, and numbers greater than 2 are used for basting stitching.

Depending on the sewing machine you will be able to choose between a certain numbers of putnadas.

Just because one sewing machine has more stitches than another does not mean it is better. Although, the more stitch options you have the better.

Reverse lever

Also known as a **reverse button**. This is used to finish off the seams. In some seams it is customary to reinforce the stitches with reverse seams.

This guarantees the resistance and total finish of the manufactured pieces. It is a very practical utility, especially when starting in sewing, and you want to ensure the quality of the garments.

Coil holder

In them the thread is located, and it is also known as **thread tension**. According to the thickness of the thread, the small thread must be adjusted, ranging from 0 to 9. The number 4 is considered normal, however, if we are dealing with a thicker or thinner thread, it requires an adjustment.

Presser foot

Having already known the needles while you place the thread, you will find the presser foot. This can be graduated through a small lever generally located at the rear of the machine. If you want to thread the thread, you must raise it, to start you must lower it. **Did you see how easy it is?**

Sewing plate

Basically it is the **base** where the presser foot and needle are located. The drive teeth are also located in this area.

Bobbin holders

It is a small **metal drawer that is** easily removable. Inside is the bobbin and thread.

Practice, the key to learning to machine sew

After the theory, practice always comes, although we will not use cloth, but paper. It is a good way not to waste fabric and learn to control the sensitivity of the machine pedal. We can print different paper templates that we can find on the Internet and prepare them for testing. We will turn on the machine and put the paper as if it were cloth. The objective is to follow the lines of the templates and do it with the machine without threading. It is normal that it takes a little work to follow all the lines, although in a short time we will master it.

The next step is to thread the machine, for this we will have to place the thread passing it through the thread guide. Many of the most modern electrical machines have drawings on it. So it won't be hard for us to thread the needle.

Winding the bobbin is the next step, which consists of filling that bobbin with thread. In this way, knots and snags in the thread are avoided. To do this, we will take out the bobbin, then we will give a few turns with the thread and we will place it. When we step on the pedal, the bobbin winder will turn and when the bobbin is full we can stop stepping on it.

Types of Sewing Machine

The first sewing machines came as furniture, with a pedal that if you pressed it constantly generated an inertia that allowed you to do the cooking work. Today the **sewing machines** are electric and the movement is carried out only by the machine.

However, they can be differentiated according to the **functionality** they have:

- **Straight nose sewing machine:** They can sew with 1, 2 and 3 needles. They make closed seams.

- **Overlock machine:** It is also known as Overlock. You can make an overcast stitch, preventing the selvedges from fraying.

- **Coating machine:** The seam of this machine is flat, and is ideal for knitting. You can do topstitching and also closed seams.

- **Collared machine:** Tape is **inserted** through a funnel, which is folded for parts of fabric with curved areas such as the neck of a shirt.

- **Bastera machine: It** makes invisible stitches that are used for hems or hems in skirts and pants.

- **Docking machine:** It is used in places where the fabric is subjected to a lot of stretching. Secure pockets.

- **Button machine:** Paste the flat buttons in all ways.

- Buttonhole **machine:** Make buttonholes and can cut them automatically.

- Closing **machine: It** makes a chain stitch with a French stitch and is used to close pants, sleeves, shirts, among others.

- Elastic **machine:** Apply elastics

- **Cutting machine: They** cut according to a pattern and the depth of a blade.

How to Choose a Sewing Machine?

Let's start at the beginning, how do I know that I am choosing the right sewing machine? Next I am going to give you some tricks to know which sewing machine to buy:

1. **What sewing level am I at?** If it is the first sewing machine that I am going to buy, the best thing is that you buy a machine that is neither too expensive nor too complex, because, when you start you do not know if you are going to like it or simply do not know if it will to give well. Also, not because it is a cheap machine means it is bad. If you are already in that phase in which you are sewing with machines of the year of your mother, or that you dust, but still and despite the difficulties of being old machines, you are good, I recommend that you buy a good machine quality but not excessively expensive. And if you are already at a very advanced level, surely you have already tried several brands, and you know more or less the brand that best suits you and the benefits you want the machine to have for the jobs you normally do.

2. **What purpose will your sewing machine have?** That is to say, you want a machine to sew your own clothes, to sew your neighbors and do some work, or you really want to dedicate yourself professionally to sewing ... It depends on the objective that the sewing machine will fulfill, so we will choose some machines with more or less motor power. You can check this in the characteristics of the machine, even look at the technical sheet on the manufacturer's page directly. If you are already professionals and the objective is industrial sewing, then do not think about it, there are many workshop machines that close and are great second-hand and at a good price.

3. **What brand do I choose?** I always say the same thing, but for me they are the best and give quality assurance, ALFA and SINGER, are my favorites. BROTHER is not bad either, and if you want them good but somewhat more expensive the JUKI are the best.

4. **Mechanical or electrical?** Well, here it will depend on tastes and how well you know about technology. The mechanics are simple, no screens, no stories, just wheels, but perhaps the benefits of making programmed or embroidered buttonholes are missing. On the other hand, the electric ones are of a higher range, most with a touch screen and tend to have more features.

5. **What do I do if I am between two similar models?** I personally before similar machines, I would choose the latest model if the brand is the same. If they are two different brands, here is a matter of taste, I am more of SINGER, but there are people who are more of Alfa. And if you have too many doubts, I would look at the power of the motor, this has a great influence on being able to sew fabrics together, denim, elastic and that the drag of the fabric is better and does not hit jumps.

What to know before buying an old sewing machine?

If you don't own an old sewing machine, but long **for these lovely pieces**, there are online stores where you can get one. First of all, you must decide if you want it for decorative purposes, for sewing or both.

Here are **some recommendations** to take into account when choosing your old sewing machine:

- For a sewing machine to be considered as old, its **manufacturing date** must be before 1900. So check its history and model well as they will help you to clearly certify the age of the machine.

- Carefully observe the materials with which it is built and the condition it is in. **Check the level of deterioration or wear** of the mechanical parts, paint and the furniture or drawer that contains it.

- **Examine the accessories,** if you have your original wooden box, manual, keys and documents. These elements increase the price of the machine.

- Although Singer is the favorite brand for its quality and history worldwide, **it is not the only brand.** You can choose from a few others such as Alpha, Pfaff or Sigma. Everything will depend on what you can find in your locality or in your search on the net.

- If you want to sew with it, remember that **the stitch type is limited.** They were first produced to make straight stitches, later those ready to zigzag and embroider flourished.

- Weight is a characteristic that you should also observe. Old sewing machines **are** generally **quite heavy** due to the materials with which they were built. Take this into consideration if you want to move it constantly.

- Make sure that your provider can offer you **maintenance service** with quality spare parts. Also find accessories that can help you keep your old sewing machine always in good condition.

Setting-up Your Machine and its Processing

Suppose you want to join two pieces of flat material. **You thread a needle** with a length of cotton (perhaps bending it to strengthen it), press the two pieces of material together, then simply push the needle through them to take the cotton with it.

You pull the needle through it, move it a bit along the material to form a stitch, then push it back through the material in the opposite direction, leaving some of the thread (the stitch) behind. In this **type of manual sewing** a single thread is used, and the stitches are alternately formed at the top and bottom of the material.

If that's your sewing idea, you've probably never been able to imagine **how a sewing machine works**. If you keep raising and lowering the needle, how can the thread pass without getting tangled?

If the needle pushes the thread down through the material and then pulls it up again, how does a stitch form? Doesn't the stitch come off when the needle goes back up? It does not make any sense! This problem challenged many inventors during the 19th century, who struggled with ways to mechanize the process used by a skilled human seamstress.

It's easy to see how a robotic arm can sew stitches, because it could hold a needle the same way you do and repeat exactly the same movements. But an ordinary sewing machine clearly can't sew that way because it never "let go" of the needle, pushes it through the material, or reverses its direction. And, in any case, they had no robots in those days.

So the secret behind sewing machines is that they work in a totally different way, using a different type of stitch and two totally separate threads, one fed from above (by the needle) and another fed from below (by a spool called coil mounted on a rotary conveyor called a shuttle).

The needle pushes the thread down through the material, forming a loop that hooks onto a hook on the shuttle. The loop wraps around the bobbin thread as the needle pulls the next section of thread through the material.

So what the needle is actually doing is repeatedly feeding the thread through the material to form successive stitches. This type of automatic sewing with two threads instead of one is called a stitch. Here are few basic principles in sewing technique

1. In principle, the machine lowers the red thread. The **wheel** turning counterclockwise grabs it and takes it away.

2. The red wire continues to rotate past the **winding** with the green wire.

3. The green wire begins to rotate clockwise.

4. When the red thread finishes turning, the **knot** is finished with the green thread and the cycle begins again, with the needle running a bit to the side.

The electric motor is supported at the bottom, at the opposite end of the machine, next to the needle. Using a pulley arrangement, drive the large flywheel on top (the wheel that can be turned to sew slowly and carefully), shown red in these diagrams, and the main power shaft (gray). Let's look at the three key mechanisms in turn.

1. NEEDLE MECHANISM

This is the simplest of the three mechanisms. The gray shaft drives a wheel (blue) and the crankshaft (green) that causes the needle (black) to go up and down. The crank converts the rotary movement of the motor (round and round) into the reciprocal movement (up and down) of the needle.

2. COIL AND SHUTTLE MECHANISM

As we will see in a moment, the shuttle and the hook that make the needle thread stitches have to rotate a little faster than the needle. Therefore, the gray shaft has to rotate the shuttle more quickly, which it can do using gears (or pulleys wrapped in round wheels of different sizes).

3. FEED TOOTH FEED MECHANISM

The conveyor moves the fabric through the machine at a constant speed, thus ensuring stitches of equal length. It works by moving up and forward at the same time, which occurs through two interconnected mechanisms that are actuated from the main shaft. I've drawn one of them (in the middle) as a cam (blue), an egg-shaped wheel that makes a lever (yellow) sway back and forth, pulling the drive tooth from right to left and then back again.

At the same time, a second crank mechanism (green and red) moves the drive tooth up and down. When these two movements are synchronized, the drive tooth works a bit like a horseshoe on the end of an upside down leg. Normally, a shoe on your leg moves down and back, then stands up and repeats the same movement, pushing back against the ground so that your body moves forward.

But a drive tooth (with the horseshoe pointing upward) moves up and forward, "walking" the material through the machine one step (one stitch!) At a time.

The Basic Stitches

When learning to machine sew for beginners, you start with the most basic stitches you can give. In this case, the simplest stitch is the one known as straight or linear. It is ideal to take our first steps with the sewing machine. To do this, we will only have to select it in the machine program. Then we will select the length we want for each of our stitches. Which should not be too short or long, we must seek that there is a middle ground.

Another very simple stitch that is used by both beginners and people who already know how to sew well by machine is the zigzag stitch. Thanks to it, the fabrics can be frayed. So after stitching something or to make sure this doesn't happen, we'll select the zigzag stitch.

As with the straight or linear stitch, we can also choose the length that it should have, with which we will be able to reinforce the edge of the seam. Although we are learning to sew, we cannot forget a point of great importance that professional people also use, the invisible hem. In this case, and as its own name indicates, it is a kind of stitch that is not very noticeable. To achieve this, you must use a thread that is the same color as the fabric, or at least as similar as possible. In this way, we can reinforce the fabric without stitching made in another color and the work will be with a much better appearance.

Sewing Machine Basic Materials

In addition to your sewing machine you will need a few tools that will make your life easier. In the haberdashery and on the websites you will find a lot of accessories, here are the main ones that we think are essential to get started:

- **A seam ripper:** this utensil is used to undo missed seams (tool widely used at the start of learning ...)
- **scissors:** embroidery scissors with thin, short and very pointed blades to cut the threads + cutting scissors with blades of at least 20 cm to ensure a good cut of your fabrics + pinking scissors so that the fabric does not fray step + paper scissors to cut the patterns.

- **Rotary Cutter:** it can be used instead of cutting scissors. It is a cutter with a round blade, which makes it very easy to cut the fabric.

- **A cutting mat:** rather take it in a large format (60 x 90 cm). It is very practical for cutting fabrics with a rotary cutter.

- **Pins:** rather thin and long so as not to damage the fabrics. A needle holder (or pin holder) is very practical for planting your pins and catching them quickly.

- **A traditional needle:** for sewing by hand, it will be useful for the finishing of certain projects.

- **Water-soluble felts (e.g. ultra-washable felts for children):** to mark your marks (seam allowances for example) on your fabrics.

- **Pattern paper (or tracing paper in large format):** to trace the pieces to be cut on the pattern boards provided in the books or for download on certain sites.

- **Safety pins:** very practical for passing elastics for example.

- **Cans:** you normally have 2-3 cans sold with your sewing machine, but they will quickly prove to be insufficient. Have a few cans in advance so you can make one can for each color of thread spool.

- **Vlieseline:** to cover your applied materials, but also to reinforce certain parts of your works which could be subjected to significant and / or repeated constraints (press studs for example).

- **A measuring tape**

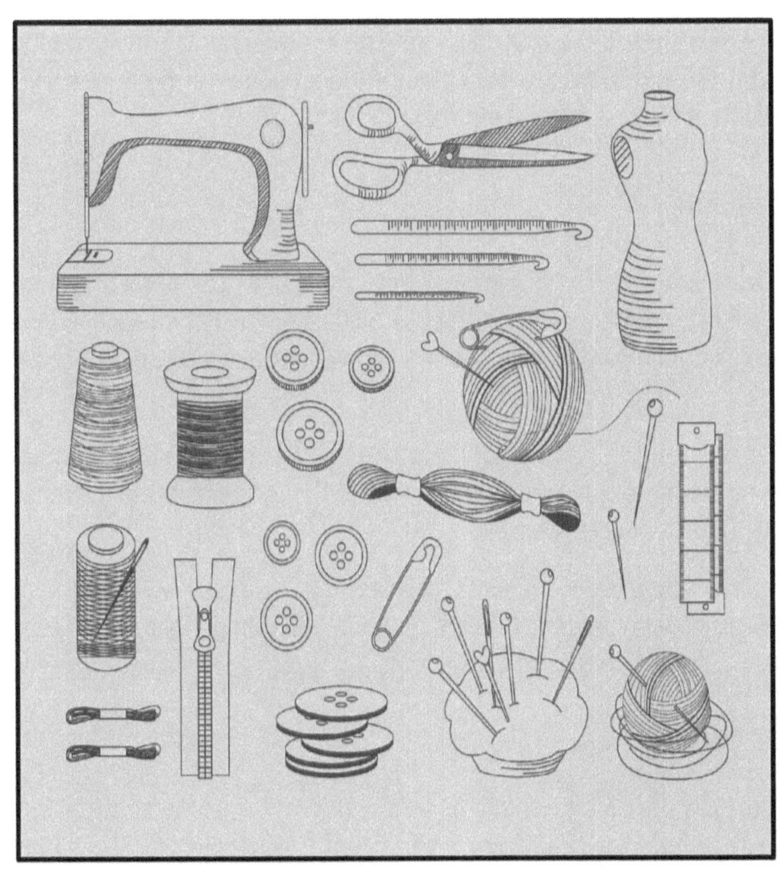

Categories of Sewing Machine Accessories

If you want to start in the charming and magical world of clothing, you must know the **sewing tools**. In the market there is a great variety of materials for the art of sewing, so you should familiarize yourself with them.

The **sewing tools** are the tools that people use to cut and make any outfit. There are those who engage in this activity as a hobby or by profession. Hence, there are some tools for use by beginners, intermediates or professionals.

So, to clarify any questions about these **sewing tools**, we invite you to read this entry until the end. Here I will explain in detail some of the accessories you will need to achieve your goals in these projects.

Added Products

There is a wide range of **sewing materials** in any physical store or online store such as Amazon. However, the choice of these utensils will depend on your sewing machine or your requirements, so we suggest you check before buying.

In the initial process with some basic **cutting and sewing materials it** is enough. Then, if you go for sewing, you will increase your material requirements to make this task easier.

Next, I will show you the **sewing tools** by categories. In this way, you will be able to identify what you really need in your workshop, managing your budget better:

1. Basic

In this category we are going to include the **sewing tools** that we consider are necessary in any workshop. So that you can detail it better, we show them to you in the following list:

- **Threads.** This material is the soul of the garments, so you must be careful when selecting it. You must have in your workshop a wide variety of colors that match the fabrics. Using a good quality thread guarantees the resistance of the seam and the smooth operation of the sewing machine.

- **Pins.** You can find very useful hook pins for attaching multiple layers of fabric while cutting. Also, there are head pins, such as patchwork pins, which, being long and thin, have different benefits.

- **Thimble.** This sewing material is used to push the needle into stiff fabrics without damaging the fingers. Therefore, it should not be missing in your sewing workshop.

- **Measuring tape.** It is used to take measurements (length, width, contours and others) or check patterns. It is essential for the seamstress or seamstress to elaborate any project. Some are made of fabric or plastic and usually measure from one to three meters, but the average length is 150cm.

- **Cloth scissors.** There are different models. Ideally, they should be comfortable, soft-handled and ergonomic, and cut well. I recommend you choose a good quality option (stainless steel) and of various sizes. With them you can cut fabrics, buttonholes, and sewing threads, customize garments and fix zippers.

- **Paper scissors.** It is required to cut the patterns on paper, so you do not use the fabric scissors, preventing them from being damaged.

- **Seam ripper.** It is a "Y" shaped sheet of metal, with a ball that protects the fabric on one end. It is used when for any reason you think the seam does not meet the requirements.

- **Sewing machine needles.** It is important to have several needles for different fabrics. These sewing instruments are cheap so you can buy several if they affect your budget a lot. You must verify that it is compatible with the sewing machines you have in the workshop and of good quality.

- **Chalks to mark**. It comes in different colors can be triangular pieces, rosillos or pencils. With them you can mark the face of the fabric that will be hidden to guide you.

- **Iron**. It is an indispensable tool, as it allows the fabric to be kept in place and provides a smooth finish when required.

- **Needles for hand sewing**. This instrument consists of a metal filament or other hard material. It usually has a straight shape and many seamstresses use it to baste the garments, before consolidating the project.

- **Sewing table**. Every seamstress should have a good sewing machine table for their machine. Regardless of your level. This to be able to sew comfortably.

2. Those that facilitate any task

Here we include the accessories that allow the project to be carried out in a **comfortable, fast and perfectly finished way**.

So that you can appreciate its benefits, we present you below a list of these **sewing and clothing materials**:

- **Bobbin case.** This tool allows you to properly organize the bobbins with different colored threads. In this way, you can have available any thread you require at the time of sewing. Ideally, it should be translucent and close the lid tightly to prevent the bobbins from falling to the floor.

- **Zigzag scissors.** They are toothed scissors also called scissors for bastille. They are used to give an uneven finish to the fabric so that it does not fray (selvedge). In addition, they are very useful to avoid overcasting in the internal finishes. They must be sharp enough so that the cut is clean and does not jam.

- **Pincushions.** Among the sewing accessories you cannot miss the pin pad, although you can buy it or make it yourself. These allow you to organize and have on hand the pins you need to use on the garment.

- **Eye-opener.** It is used to loosen or open buttonholes. You can find it in industrial or domestic format, the latter usually comes with sewing machines.

- **Girabies.** It consists of a thin needle-like instrument, with a hook on one end and a circle on the other, used to turn the bias or narrow strips of fabric.

- **Automatic thread threader.** There are some machines that have this system included, but the older ones do not have it. However, it can be purchased separately, it is very useful and easy to use, it will facilitate the arduous task of threading the thread in the machine.

- **Tweezers.** It is also useful for threading the thread in machines or overlocker and removing excess threads in fabrics.

- **Basting thread.** It is a special type of thread that is used for the previous work of the garments.

- **Rules for sewing.** They allow accurate measurements and strokes on fabrics and paper to make patterns. There are different straight, curved, square, square and other models.

3. Accessories for professional seamstresses

These **sewing and tailoring materials** include a multitude of accessories that in many cases are purchased as a set. A workshop for professional seamstresses has higher demands than a beginner's. It even requires special sewing machines such as embroidery machines, overlockers and others.

Next, I will mention some accessories that you will need as a professional:

- **Rotary cutter.** It is a fabric cutter, it is not a basic tool, but it is very useful in your workshop. It saves time because it makes clean cuts quickly. It's great for straight cuts, but if you have experience you can even make curved cuts.

- **Cutting base.** It is a special tool to use the cutter, it is self-healing, cheap and very practical, they will also extend the life of your cutter. We suggest you organize a cutting station in your workshop to carry out this activity.

- **Presser foot kit.** Sewing machines usually come with various types of presser feet. But, you can buy other sets of these instruments for different types of seams and get creative.

- **Mannequin.** This instrument is necessary to present the patterns of the projects or garments in process and once completed. It is very useful to make the final adjustments of the pieces.

- **Dressmaking gauge.** It is used to make small measurements, you can help with it in the hem seam or to mark buttonholes.

- **Ironing center.** It is a sophisticated, but highly operational tool for smoothing fabrics. It consists of a kettle with an iron. It has more power than a normal iron. It has a higher vapor pressure giving a professional result.

- **Seam box.** It is an accessory that serves as an organizer. Very practical for the seamstress because there you can have thread, needles, bobbin holder or other instrument that you may need while working.

- **Tailor scissors.** They have an adequate physical structure with a perfect balance between mango and leaves. One of the rings is oval in shape and larger, offering comfort when gripping them. Allows for precise cuts and long-lasting cutting edge.

- **Sewing book.** They are books with well-defined instructions and patterns that can be useful to complete any project.

- **Pattern weights.** They are tools to keep patterns in place, both made of fabric and paper, you can easily make them at home.

Sewing Kits

In the market there is a wide range **of sewing games** presented to users in kit. So, the user gets the main accessories in one product. But, if you are starting in the world of sewing you may be asking yourself the following:

What they are and what do they contain?

Sewing kits are **cut and** sew **material kits** that come in a box. Its usefulness is to support the seamstress or seamstress in their work, such as repairing a garment, making a hem or customizing a piece.

Its content may vary, but basically it must have **essential sewing tools**. So that you can build yours in an easy and practical way, I will show you the materials in the following list:

- Coils of thread.

- Needle threader.

- Buttons.

- Seam ripper.

- Measuring tape.

- Pins.

- Needles

- Safety pins

- Pincushions.

With these sewing materials you can get out of any trouble at any given time. However, you can find different types of sewing kit in physical stores or online like **Amazon**.

There is a beginner's **kit, a professional sewing** kit and even a children's sewing kit. The tools included in each sewing set are adapted to the needs of the interested user.

The **professional kit** should include all material sewing a tailor may need at some point. In addition to the aforementioned materials, it must include other tools that allow for more complex work, such as certain presser feet.

As for the **children's kits, they** are intended to motivate their creativity and interest in sewing. For this, some stores include stuffed animals, cushions of some type of fabric to be sewn. In addition, they add dresses, an explanatory manual, fabrics, garters and others.

The quality of the kit will stand out for the **quantity and quality of its components**. In this way, it guarantees the seamstress to carry out more complex projects and greater durability of the material.

Recommendations for Sewing Kits

It is important that both the **bag and briefcase is made of a hard material** to protect internal tools.

Likewise, it is necessary that the instruments are **sectioned and well supported** (elastic tape) to prevent them from moving during any transfer. Thus, each element will remain organized, without the risk of damage.

The quality of needles and threads is essential to work on any sewing machine or with manual arrangements. For this reason, **I recommend checking the quality of each tool before purchasing the kit.**

The Basics of Sewing Thread & Fabric

After reading the content under this heading you will know exactly what thread to buy for your sewing machine. Keep reading so that you know exactly what type of thread to choose and you won't make the mistake of hundreds of people who buy the wrong thread and end up throwing their money away.

Sewing or **sewing threads** are very thin bodies that are obtained through textile processes. The function of a thread is to provide aesthetics and good performance in sewing and stitches.

When buying a new sewing machine you are going to want to make sure you buy the right thread to get the most out of it.

There are three types of yarn based on their origin of raw materials: **plants, animals and synthetic.** The threads from plants such as cotton and linen, their resistance is not very strong.

Those originating from animal fibers are those of natural silk and wool from sheep. These guys are very strong and resistant.

You will find sewing machine threads in different presentations, **different sizes, thicknesses and colors.** Overlock or Overlock threads come specifically in a cone shape, and depending on the machine, you will need multiple cones.

Properties of Thread

- Strength to tension

- Tenacity

- Strength

- Loop minimum strength

- Elongation at break

- Module

- Elasticity

- Shrinkage

- Moisture gain

Types of Thread

Since there are types of seams, there are also various **types of sewing threads**. Choosing a good thread will ensure that your sewing machine does not break the thread. Next, I will tell you about the most frequent types of threads that you will find in a haberdashery:

Thread photo	Thread type	Description
	General-purpose thread	They are the most used to sew various garments, curtains, among others. They are characterized by sewing everything, and you can use it to sew by hand or as a thread for a sewing machine. They're made of polyester, which are strong and great for sewing jobs looking for sagging threads. And cotton, they are ideal for any type of

fabric and lingerie work.

	Extra strong thread	They are used in fabric furniture such as upholstery and curtains. They are made of polyester or cotton. Also combined in polyester and cotton.
	Embroidery thread	It is a thread that is made of polyester and in some cases Rayon, they are shiny and reflect in the light. You can also find them with a matte finish, they are used to make embroidery.
	Silk thread	This type of thread is ideal for sewing wool or silk fabrics. Although it is not economical, it is recommended that you use it in this type of fabric. You can also use it to sew by hand, as it is easy to use and does not tangle. It is a fine, shiny and soft fiber.
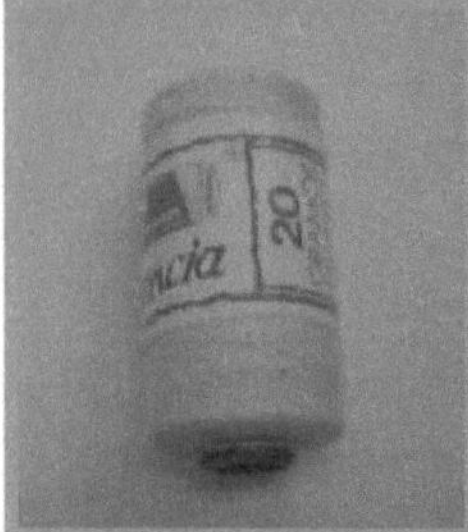	Basting thread	It is made of cotton. It is ideal for basting by hand before passing the garment through the machine. It is not advisable to use for final machine seams.

It is a very strong and thick thread. It is used when you need to give volume to a

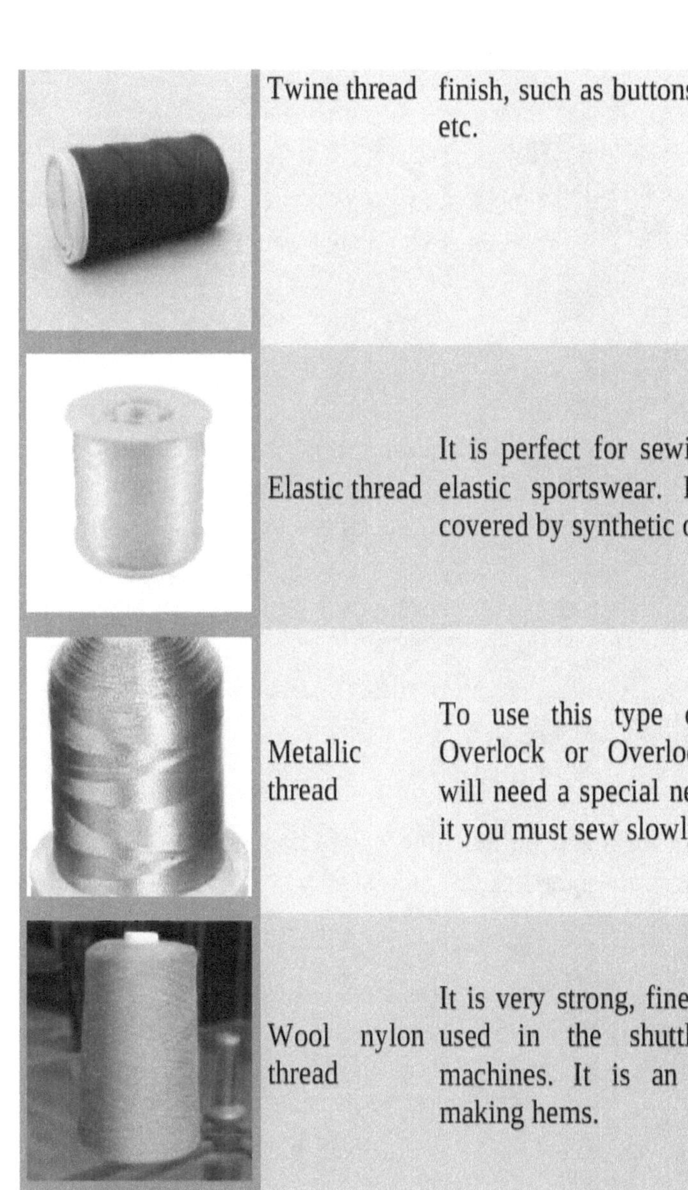

	Twine thread	finish, such as buttons, finishing seams, etc.
	Elastic thread	It is perfect for sewing a swimsuit or elastic sportswear. It usually comes covered by synthetic or natural fiber.
	Metallic thread	To use this type of thread on an Overlock or Overlock machine, you will need a special needle. When using it you must sew slowly and constantly.
	Wool nylon thread	It is very strong, fine and smooth. It is used in the shuttles of Overlock machines. It is an ideal thread for making hems.
	Bobbin filled thread	It is very fine and is used in sewing machines for embroidery. They are usually only in white or black, although other colors are currently available.

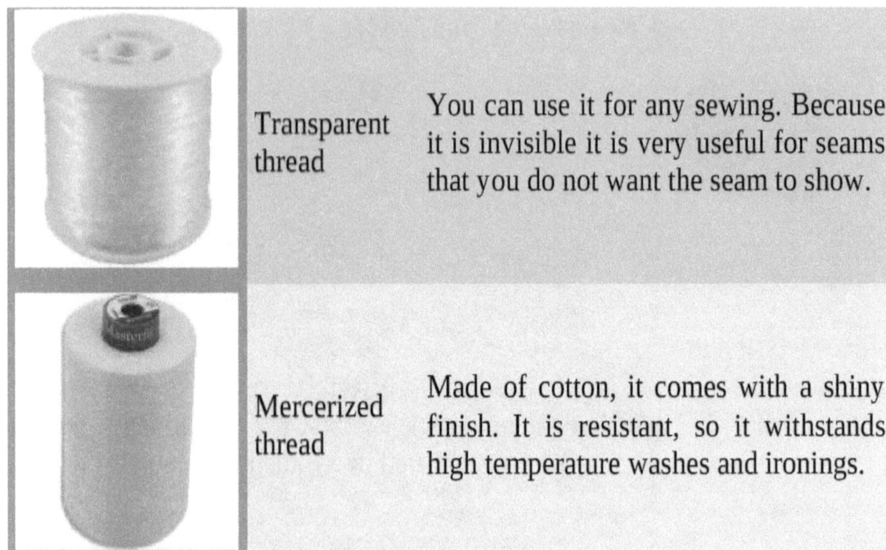

	Transparent thread	You can use it for any sewing. Because it is invisible it is very useful for seams that you do not want the seam to show.
	Mercerized thread	Made of cotton, it comes with a shiny finish. It is resistant, so it withstands high temperature washes and ironings.

Selecting Appropriate Thread

Choosing the **thread for a sewing machine** is very important for you to do a good sewing job. Here are some tips that will be very useful:

Seam type

Depending on the type of sewing you are going to make, you will choose which thread you need, whether it should be resistant or simple. Determine the purpose of the seam, whether it is a decorative or functional garment.

Yarn characteristics

After knowing the types of threads that exist, you must determine which one you need. According to its classification you will know if you require a fine thread, which is used for delicate fabrics that do not need as much resistance.

Also, a standard thread, which is the most used for clothing work. A thick thread, used for sturdier seems like buttons, zippers, or thick fabrics.

Thread appearance

Check that the thread strand is clean. If you notice that the strands have protruding hairs, it is better not to use that thread.

Thread thickness

Another point that you should also take into account before choosing the right thread is its thickness. There are three types of thread thickness for over lockers and sewing machines:

- Twisted thread, which is a very thick thread

- Normal thread, it is ideal for all types of seams

- Extra fine thread, it is perfect for sewing delicate fabrics and embroidery.

- Here I leave you the **nomenclature of the threads in terms of thickness**. It is made up of two numbers, the first one referring to the stretches that are made when it was made. The second indicates the number of strands that form it.

- **Very Thick** 40/3: High resistance seams.

- **Thick** 40/2

- **Medium** 70/2 and 60/2: Sew fabrics such as Denim, Poplin or similar fabrics.

- **Slim** 100/2: Sewing children's clothing.

- **Very Thin** 120/2: Embroider lace or light fabrics.

Choose the color

Choosing the thread color **will depend on the shade of the fabric**. For this, I advise you to take a sample of the fabric when buying the thread. It must match the fabric you will be using. In this way, the seam will be more integrated and will not be seen with the naked eye.

There are a wide variety of thread colors, making it easy to choose the right color for your sewing job.

Brands and quality

Acquire good quality threads. The sewing takes a lot of dedication and time so don't save when choosing the thread. Sewing with a poor quality thread is horrible, it can break and you will not get good results.

If you choose a good brand of insurance it is a quality thread. There are many recognized brands such as Gutermann or Mettle. They offer good yarns with a variety of colors and tones.

- If you are looking to achieve **optimal results,** I suggest using:

- **Polyester** thread for use in synthetic fabrics.

- **Cotton** thread for use on natural fabrics.

- **Polyester** thread for use in mixed fabrics, that is, polyester and cotton.

Among other **tips** you can also consider are the following:

Use the same thread for the needle and the bobbin for the overlocker or sewing machine. This in order that there are no differences between both stitches and the result will be uniform.

When you choose a thread, you must make sure that it is the one **indicated for the over locker or sewing machine.**

If you use a lot a lot, you can choose to buy this thread in cones. It is much more profitable.

If you take into account these tips we have given you, choosing the thread for sewing will be much easier. Just **adjust the stitch tension** your machine needs and you can start sewing.

What type of overlock thread to use?

The **thread serger** is an essential element in the world of sewing. It is a material that you can choose according to the type of garment you are going to sew. Without a doubt, it is the main element to fix any type of fabric.

Choosing a sewing thread can sometimes seem less important. A quality thread will make **the sewing result excellent** and durable.

Overlock or overlock thread is slightly thinner than that used on sewing machines. This type of thread prevents bulky seams from coming together and pulling. Using multiple spools of thread ensures that the final seam, hem, or finish is flexible and strong.

If you want to know more about this topic, I invite you to continue reading until the end of this post. You dare?

Where to buy threads for overlock?

Buying through online stores is one of the best options that exists today. You can access a wide range of options, prices, discounts and promotions from anywhere in the world.

You can also buy this type of thread in an online store. They offer you a large number of thread brands of different types, excellent quality and various colors. They are sold individually or in combos.

Finally, the thread is a fundamental part for you to use your overlocker. Choosing the correct type of thread has direct consequences on your sewing work. For this reason, you should choose quality threads that have varieties of colors that adapt to any fabric.

The Basics of Presser Feet

Presser feet are one of the most important and versatile tools that make up sewing machines. These, in their great majority are usually very cheap, in addition to having a wide range of various **types of presser feet**. Which have the functionality to simplify and save time in sewing work, thus allowing quality finishes.

Currently, there is a marked lack of knowledge regarding the appropriate types and uses of each of the presser feet. **Continue reading** this article, and **know everything related to the different types of presser feet**.

Types of Presser Feet

There are many presser feet on the market, so we will mention 6 **types of presser feet and what they are for**.

Photo of presser foot	Name	Description
	Basic presser foot	The presser foot that is incorporated par excellence in sewing machines, is known as the basic presser foot. These presser feet are generally used for simple and versatile sewing, such as quilting, zigzag and straight stitch designs.
	Zipper foot	There are many presser feet available for zippers, even these can also be sewn with a simple presser foot. However, it is impossible to obtain the same results compared to special presser feet for sewing on zippers. Since these are designed, they are used to sew the zippers, bringing the seam closer to it

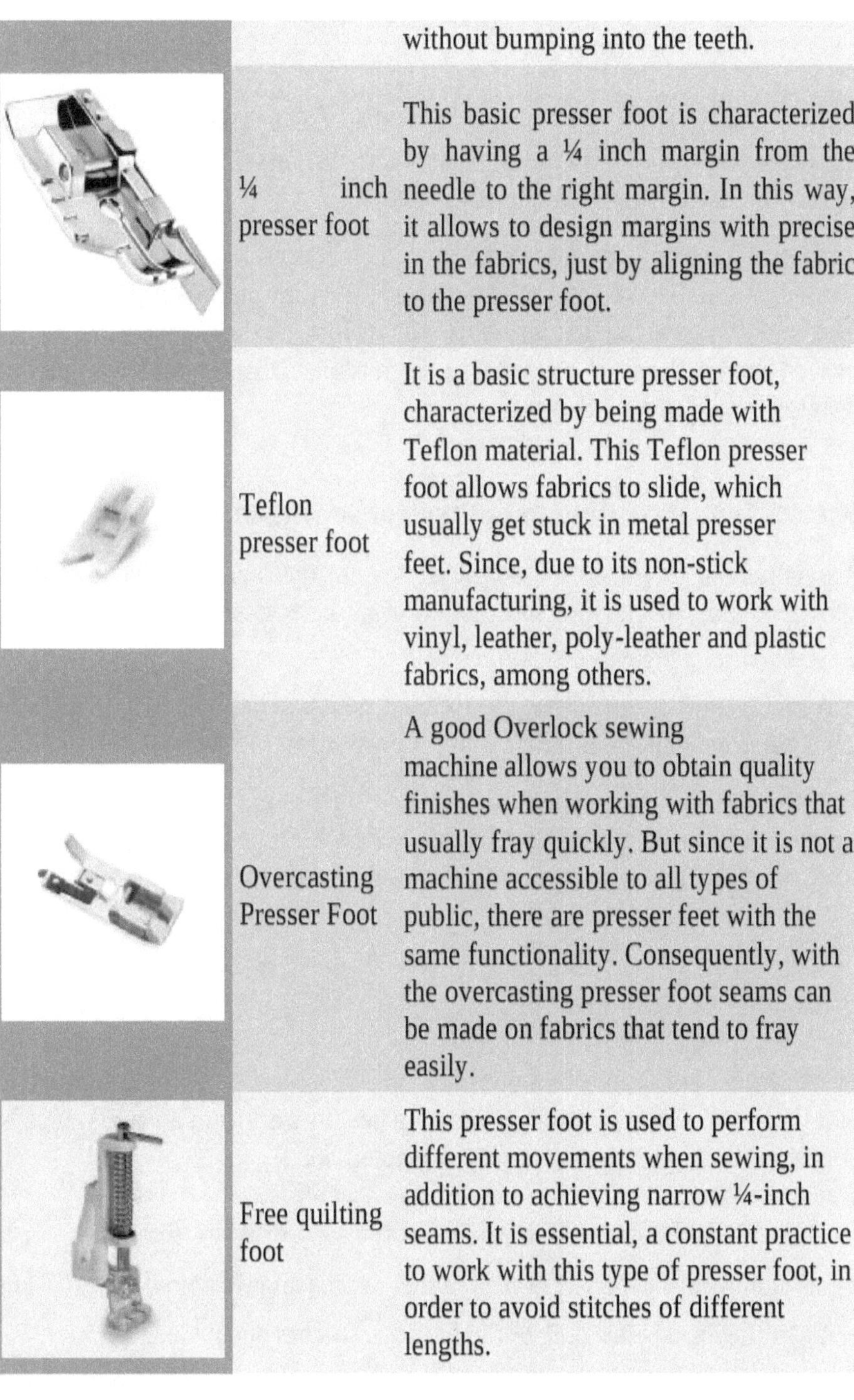

without bumping into the teeth.

¼ inch presser foot	This basic presser foot is characterized by having a ¼ inch margin from the needle to the right margin. In this way, it allows to design margins with precise in the fabrics, just by aligning the fabric to the presser foot.
Teflon presser foot	It is a basic structure presser foot, characterized by being made with Teflon material. This Teflon presser foot allows fabrics to slide, which usually get stuck in metal presser feet. Since, due to its non-stick manufacturing, it is used to work with vinyl, leather, poly-leather and plastic fabrics, among others.
Overcasting Presser Foot	A good Overlock sewing machine allows you to obtain quality finishes when working with fabrics that usually fray quickly. But since it is not a machine accessible to all types of public, there are presser feet with the same functionality. Consequently, with the overcasting presser foot seams can be made on fabrics that tend to fray easily.
Free quilting foot	This presser foot is used to perform different movements when sewing, in addition to achieving narrow ¼-inch seams. It is essential, a constant practice to work with this type of presser foot, in order to avoid stitches of different lengths.

Presser foot classification

Normal: they are those presser feet that come assembled on sewing machines through a screw mechanism. Normal presser feet generally found on sewing machines are not that advanced.

Snap-on: these presser feet have a built-in lever on the back that when pressed allows them to be assembled to the machine. The modern machines are manufactured with this type of foot, so they replace the normal foot. In another sense, if you want to use machines that do not have Snap-on features, you must use adapters.

Presser foot according to the type of sewing machine

It is important to consider the type of sewing machine in order to make a correct choice of the presser foot. Since, these depend on the type of machines you have at home, workshop or business.

Advanced sewing machines: the rods are generally tall and 1.5 centimeters tall. Therefore, you should use a low-cut presser foot.

Traditional sewing machines: these machines are characterized in their structure by having a black head and a flat base. Its rods have a height of 2 centimeters, therefore, it is necessary to use adapters for low-cut presser feet.

Functions of Presser Feet

Every seamstress should be up-to-date on the subject **of presser foot types and their use**. Since, this allows knowing how to work with a varied range of presser feet according to the work you want to do.

- Double drag: gives a second upper drag to the fabric as a complement to the lower drag that the machines naturally exert. Thus allowing a better drag of the fabric as stitches are made.

- Invisible Doubles: Invisible hem presser feet are used to hide seam stitching.

- Roller - This type of presser foot is ideal for delicate non-slip fabrics that don't slip easily.

- Patchwork: ideal for creating multiple narrow seams with a diameter of up to 5 millimeters. In addition, it has a recess that works as a guide to measure distances of 1/8 of an inch to sew in the corners.

- Invisible zipper: they are used to avoid the visibility of the teeth of the zippers.

- Buttons: Button presser feet are ideal when you need to sew a number of buttons.

- Buttonholes: This presser foot has the utility of sewing perfect buttonholes of different sizes

- Hems: it is a presser foot used for those seams that involve making hems. With this presser foot you will try to avoid manual bends.

- Ruching: it is characterized by gathering in a decorative way simulating a series of folds or corrugated in the seams.

- For Bias Tapes: This presser foot helps to sew bias tapes, they are classified into funnel and adjustable tapes. The presser feet for applying adjustable tapes have various universal measurements. And the presser feet to apply funnel tapes do not regulate the tape they just cut and fold the bias alone.

- Satin: These presser feet allow uniform stitching on familiar fabrics with satin and satin.

- Decorative cord: it is implemented to make seams with decorative cords, without these being intertwined when sewn. The number of laces you want to sew in an instant will depend on the channels that the presser foot has.

- Monograms: Its use is based on embroidery stitches, since the central part of the presser foot has a slit. Which facilitates the sliding work of thick stitches, so as not to create lumps when passing through the presser foot.

Manufacturer sewing machine foot

If you like to work with quality materials and recognized brands, you are in the right place. **Continue reading** the next section, and you will find the presser feet according to the manufacturers of the most recognized brands. It should be noted that the brands mentioned also manufacture various **types of industrial presser feet.**

Singer

The singer brand is known for its diversity in sewing machines, whether for domestic, professional or industrial use. Among the different products that have been manufactured by this renowned brand is the presser foot.

This presser foot kit is designed to be adapted and functional for all machines of singer origin and the like. This type of presser foot mimics the functions of an overlock machine, as it trims off excess fabric.

Alpha

We will introduce you to a series of presser feet that are alpha manufactured, and adaptable to all alpha sewing machines.

- Teflon presser foot.

- Presser foot with wheels.

- Embroidery foot.

- Gathering foot

- Edging presser foot.

- Open foot for festoons.

- Decorative cord foot.

- Free closed and open quilting presser foot.

- Alpha presser foot for normal and invisible zippers.

- Double-drag closed-foot, high-sleeve foot.

- Open and closed double drag presser foot with low sleeve.

Bernina

Bernina covers the vast majority of presser feet for its manufacture, being adaptable to machines with systems similar to bernina.

- Embroidery foot.

- Trailed foot.

- Top feed presser foot.

- BRS free quilting foot.

- Presser foot for thick and thin fabrics.

- Presser foot for parallel, uniform, fine eyelashes.

- Scallop foot, decorative stitching, hems.

- Buttonhole foot, buttons, visible and invisible zippers,

Brother

Among other manufacturers that join the list of brands with quality presser foot designs. They are the Brother, which make the ideal presser feet for each type of clothing to obtain, in this way, jobs with professional finishes.

- Pearl presser foot.

- Hem foot.

- Presser foot for elastic fabrics.

- Presser foot for pipe tapes.

- Presser foot for two layers of seams.

- Presser foot for stitches and invisible zippers.

-

Bernette

Bernette has expanded its range to 10 precise presser feet to offer the possibility of making all the seams you imagine. Likewise, it facilitates work and can be used both on Bernette sewing machines and other similar machines.

- Embroidery foot.
- Overlock presser foot.
- Patchwork presser foot.
- Lacing foot.
- Gathering foot.
- Straight stitch foot.
- Open presser foot for embroidery.
- Invisible zipper foot.
- Free and darned quilting presser foot.
- Sliding sole presser foot for zigzag.

Sometimes it is advisable to invest in a presser foot kit since they save you money and you have the advantage of having different presser feet at your disposal for all your sewing projects at home.

The Basics of Patchwork Stitches

Would you like to learn some **basic patchwork points**? Currently this technique is being widely used to decorate clothes, make beautiful crafts and other details at home. Although its origins go back to ancient Egypt, today in full modernity, the economy leads to the **need to reinvent itself**.

Currently making patchwork has become a novelty and fashion. It allows you to increase your creativity, and even the possibility of starting a business starting by learning a few **simple steps**.

Best of all, you don't need high sewing skills to **create wonderful pieces**. There are some techniques that do not include sewing, using glue and other materials to create. The essential thing is to have the disposition and imagination and disposition to create.

What is patchwork?

Patchwork is an **artistic way** of sewing. You know what it means? It is literally working with patches, which can be made of different fabrics. It consists of the union of pieces obtained from scraps of fabric, which may no longer be used.

Pieces of fabric of different shapes, sizes and colors are cut, combined by applying the shape you want. These creations range from **personal**

accessories to details for the home that can be very useful.

The pieces can be joined by hand sewing, machine sewing or even gluing. In this way a harmony is achieved in the piece that is being created. The trick is to **use your imagination,** since great sewing skills are not necessary.

Perfection is achieved through practice and knowledge of **patchwork basics**. Dare to create different pieces with different uses at home. Some examples are blankets, bathroom pieces, rugs, towels, kitchen pieces. Even for personal use, ties, headbands, scarves, pins, purses, bags, everything you can think of.

Your main weapon will be creativity and the desire to start designing and making.

How to patchwork?

To do patchwork, creativity is a fundamental element, which will lead you to **create new pieces**. However, you will need to know sewing basics and some **patchwork** techniques.

It is important **to previously have the idea** of what you want to capture. For this I recommend that you gather pieces of recycled fabric, harmonize the colors and textures depending on the use you will give to your work.

Plus, make precise strokes and cuts, combining shapes - it's **all a matter of imagination!**

Patchwork by Hand

The patchwork is mostly made by hand, such work is truly enjoyable, and worth enjoying.

To make patchwork by hand you need: a pattern or pattern, easy erase marker, ruler, pins, **needle, thread and scissors**. I recommend using cotton thread and special thread to make appliques.

Another detail that you should take into account is **the surface** where you are going to work. Create a surface or work table, you can do it with wood. This will undoubtedly facilitate your cutting and assembly work.

Initially place the fabric on the wrong side, on the work table, trace with the marker the model you want. It is recommended to leave 0.5 cm when tracing to **facilitate cutting and sewing** of the piece. Combine the colors and designs of the pieces of fabric to use according to the design to be made.

It proceeds to cut the pieces and previously performs a pre-assembly of them. This will give you an idea of your design and allow you to correct some detail before sewing.

Confront the piece face to face on the right side, to start sewing, the seam will be on the wrong side. It is good that you help yourself with pins to hold the piece. I recommend using neutral colored threads such as beige, especially if the fabric is colorful or patterned.

Even though **the stitch should not be noticed,** if this happens it will not make the piece look bad. For this type of sewing I recommend the hemstitch stitch, make it on the line that you drew previously. Try to apply the same spaces between rough and rough to avoid deformities.

Little by little, put **the pieces together until the end of** your work. When finished, iron your finished work so that it can have a perfect finish.

Patchwork techniques

When you study patchwork the first time, it may be difficult at first impression, but nothing is further from this. With **practice, PROVISION** n **and the basics** of the patchwork you can create great works.

There are various patchwork techniques from the simplest to the most complex. The trick is in practice, however, don't rule out the possibility of creating your own technique. Remember that this is an art where **creativity is the main element.**

The wonderful thing about basic patchwork techniques is that you can combine them to make original and wonderful creations. I invite you to meet them.

- Grandmother's flower garden

This wonderful technique consists of **joining figures or hexagonal appliques**, which must be combined between colors and patterns. It is widely used to create flowers, hearts, however you can use it in the model or piece you want.

- Application (I applied)

This technique can be done **by first creating the desired model** in a pattern. Then you draw on the fabric, cut out and join the pieces. Once the design is obtained, you place the applique on a base piece that you want to decorate. It can be used to decorate aprons, sweaters, gloves, towels etc.

- Dresden Plate

It consists of the **union of the pieces in the form of a circle**, the cuts can be made with the combination of various geometric figures according to your taste, which start from the center of the design.

- Quilt making

It is a technique that **is accompanied by the padding** of the design. This technique is widely used to make quilts, quilts or those pieces that are intended to protect from the cold.

I already showed you some of the basic techniques for patchwork, all you need to do is decide when to start and let's get to work!

Patchwork stitches

Stitches are another aspect to consider to achieve an impeccable result in the creation of your patchwork. It is important to use a needle and thread suitable for the work to be performed.

There are sewing stitches to join the pieces of your patchwork and others to decorate and distinguish your work. The basic stitch is the most used for simple seams. The hidden point is used to fix pieces to a base, for example those that have sticky paper. Stem stitch is used to highlight edges of figures.

Machine patchwork sewing

Although patchwork is often done by hand, **it is also done by machine,** providing a faster finish. Of course, it requires more skill and care to avoid damaging the work, for this you will need good quality threads and needles.

Avoid making very **tight or very short** seams so that if you need to undo it will not be so difficult. It is advisable to review and iron what you are cooking, so you will be sure that the work is going perfectly.

Tips Patchwork for beginners

If you are attracted to this technique but you are not yet practicing it or you are debuting, keep in mind the following tips.

It is important that you become **familiar with the terms** used in this practice. This will help you to develop better in the creation of your crafts.

Arm yourself with your **belongings to work.** Pair your basket with basic utensils to make your creations. Scissors, scraps of fabric, tape measure, needles, threads of different colors, buttons, tapes, closures, are the most necessary implements. Everything will depend on the piece that we are going to create.

The sewing machine is not a must at first, unless you want to create a large piece like a quilt. Generally beginners of patchwork **start with small pieces such** as cushions, rugs, kitchen decorations with hand sewing.

Create models or patterns, or look for some that serve as a template for your designs. These can be drawings and shapes made of different materials that make your job easier. They can be cardboard, cardboard, acetate, which allow you to make cuts and shapes with precision.

The transcendent thing is that **you do not stop**, arm yourself with your work tools and start creating.

Creating Patchwork Figures

Ingenuity will take you where you cannot imagine, and you can create the **patchwork figures** you want. The geometric figures are the most used and you can combine them in an incredible way.

From them you can even create other figures such as animals, landscapes, hearts, etc. Patchwork figures are widely **used to give sight and beauty** to various garments.

Finally, to do the **basic patchwork you** need to feel confident in yourself to create what you imagine. It is advisable to review some proposals in magazines and other media. Knowing the **basic points of patchwork** will give you the necessary tools to start creating.

Remember that you will gain the skills and abilities of patchwork with practice. Check in your closet or closet and recycle all those fabrics, pieces and pieces that you do not use so that you can make fantastic combinations.

Be sure to put into practice the **basic points of patchwork** to create great crafts.

Basic Clothing Techniques

CUT & SEW

DESCRIPTION

The cut & sew technique is the easiest method to make a garment. Shapes are obtained from a single panel and cut according to the measurements of the patterns. The pieces can be created from fabrics obtained with rectilinear or circular machines for knitwear.

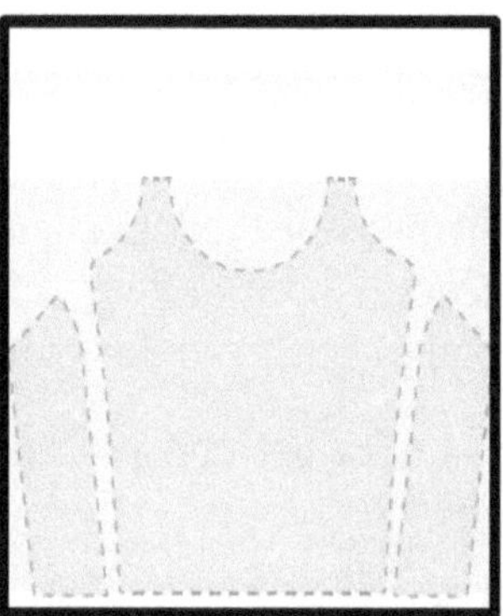

HOW DOES IT WORK

To make the garment, the pieces are joined by sewing.

ADVANTAGE

- Speed and ease of creation of knitwear.

- Ease for assembly and for the subsequent creation of the garment.

- Possibility of assembling totally different parts created with different processes.

DISADVANTAGES

- The cut piece must be sewn to prevent fraying.

- The seams can be quite obvious.

- The waste of material during the cut can be up to 25%.

- The perceived quality of garments made with this method may be low.

FULLY FASHIONED

DESCRIPTION

Garment totally edged.

HOW DOES IT WORK

The garment is shaped by the machine, which works more in some points than in others. The garment is made by creating an unbreakable chain that closes the different parts so that the fabric cannot be frayed.

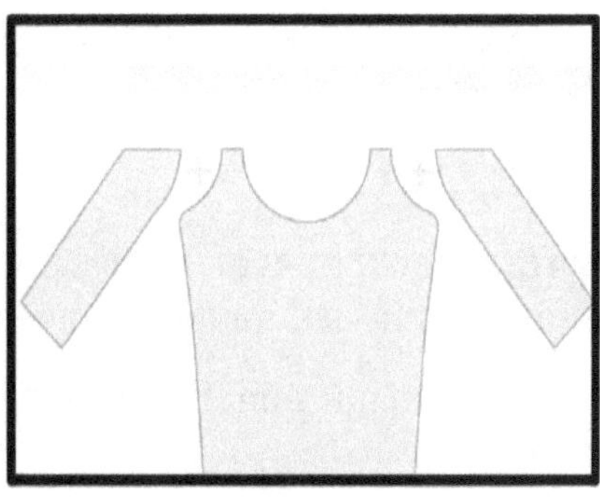

ADVANTAGE

- There is no waste due to cutting the fabric.

- The production of the form is accurate.

- The process is programmable and, therefore, repeatable, so that defects are prevented.

The processes are reduced, compared to the Cut & Sew method.

DISADVANTAGES

- Program the machine and points to prevent defects.

COMPLETE GARMENT

DESCRIPTION

With this technique, the machine produces fully formed garments, without the need for more seams.

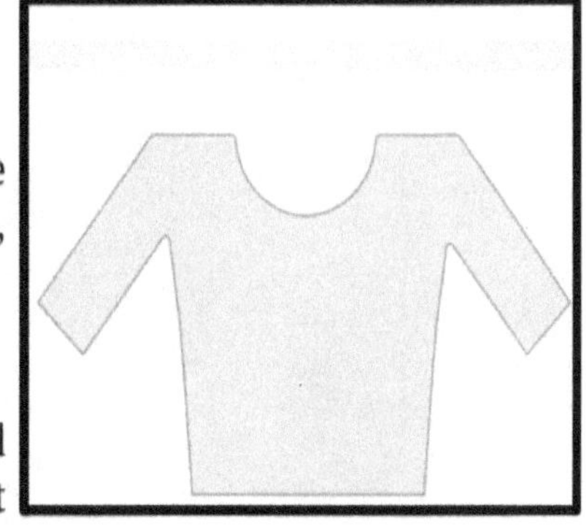

HOW DOES IT WORK

Regarding the fully fashioned elaboration, which works in 2D, it adds the possibility of making a complete three-dimensional garment. Unlike fully fashioned, where profiled pieces must be sewn together, straight knit garments are seamless. Hundreds of needles move to build and connect different tubular shapes and create a complete garment in a single production phase.

ADVANTAGE

- Further reduction of material consumption, even with respect to the fully fashioned method, since seam allowances are eliminated.

- Garment made and finished by the machine, without successive operations.

- There are no seams: aesthetic and functional advantage.

- Precise and repeatable production, correct shape and measurements, the pieces are always the same.

- Post-process reduction: zero cuts, selvedges and other applications.

DISADVANTAGES

- Program the machine and points to prevent defects.

The Basics of Sewing

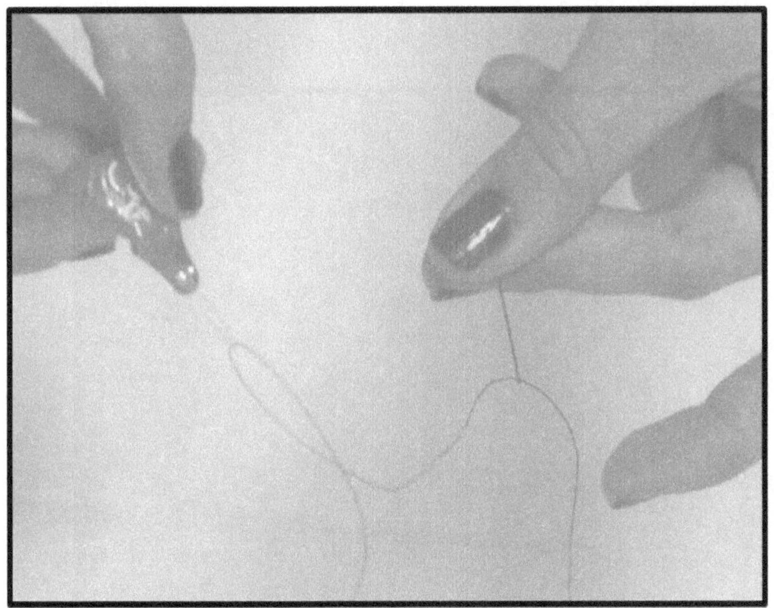

1. Threading the needle.

To thread the needle, I always follow three basic steps:

1. Make a diagonal cut with the scissors at the end of the thread that we are going to use.

2. Although it may seem a bit strange for beginners, I wet the end of the thread with saliva. I have the image of my grandmother with her glasses, her needle in one hand and with the thread hanging between her lips.

3. Insert the end of the thread through the hole in the needle. Trick: place the needle at eye level, and close one to get the best guess.

This method is the oldest in the world and the most used, but if these steps seem complicated, we have a **threader** in our hands, with this tool you will surely have no problem. You only have to introduce the metallic threads through the hole of the needle, then we put the thread there, and then we remove the threader from the needle.

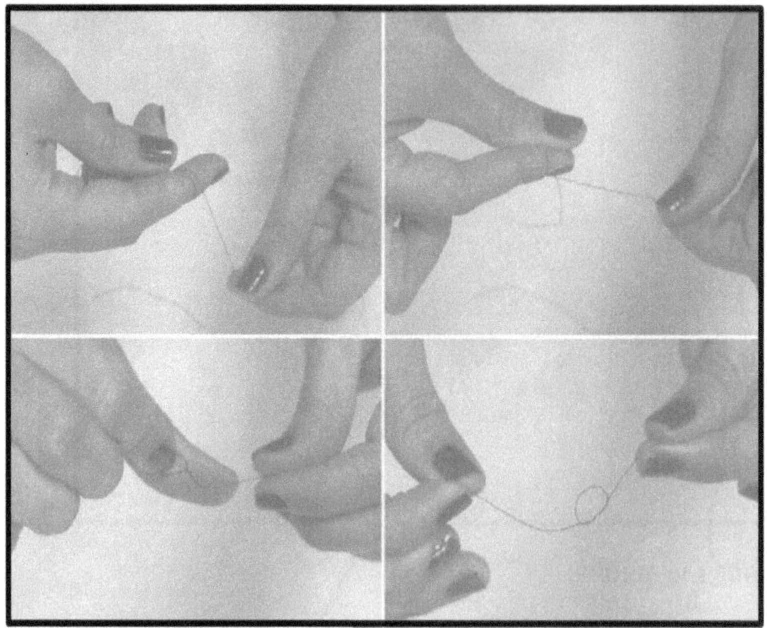

2. Knot at the end of the thread.

Always remember that you are going to sew by hand, tie a knot at the end of the thread so that it does not come off. A very easy way to do it is to wind the end of the thread on the index finger, hold it with your thumb, and then slide one finger over the other, until the thread is wound in a circle, then pull the end of the thread and you will have the knot.

3. Cut the fabric.

Cutting the fabric correctly is the first step so that our tasks are perfect. All we need is a ruler, preferably a bevel, a tailor's soap, and good dressmaker scissors (those with an ergonomic handle are more comfortable and easier to handle).

The edges of fabrics or fabrics are called selvedges. The fabrics are made of threads that intersect. When we go to cut the fabric, it is very important to take into account the direction of the thread. To know which the direction of the thread is, it is enough to know 'which is the edge of the fabric', so that we understand each other, it is the edge of the fabric that we are not cut in the store.

We will use the tape measure to know how much fabric we need, mark directly on the wrong side of the fabric with the tailor's soap or marking soap. Do not worry about the traces that remain on the fabric, once you wash the fabric there will be no trace!

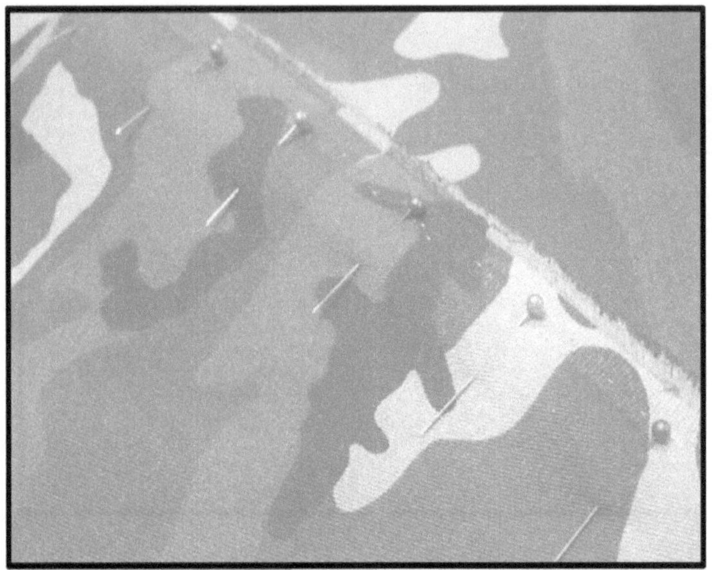

Place the pins and baste.

Before sewing two fabrics, they must be joined with pins and tacked together.

Place the edges of the fabrics together and pin them, along the fabric, about 1.5 cm from the edge. Between each pin there should be about 5 cm of separation, or even more in fabrics that are rigid.

Fabrics are basted together to hold together while sewing by hand or machine. You can use ordinary thread or special thread for basting. If you use to baste a thread of a different color from the fabric, then it will be easier to remove it when you see it better.

We can only put on the thimble and start sewing.

Initial Steps to Machine Sewing

Already knowing what the parts of a sewing machine are, you can begin to take your first steps in this wonderful world. I tell you what they are:

Mastering the pedal

A very effective technique to start mastering the pedal is to **work on paper**. Yes, as you read it, "on paper". This will allow you to train both on the pedal and on the rhythm. I recommend you do some template printing on zigzag, circles, straight lines and simple drawings and start sewing. Of course, you do not need to thread the machine, it is only a previous training without spending resources.

Denavar the bobbin

The process of winding the bobbin is to **fill the bobbin** with thread. It involves removing the bobbin, turning the thread and inserting it. Once you step on the pedal, the bobbin winder will turn and the bobbin will fill up, when this happens we can stop pressing the pedal. This process is important, since it prevents the thread and the hooks from having knots.

The first stitches

The most basic stitches are:

1. **Linear or straight: it** is considered one of the easiest to start sewing by machine. To do this, you just have to choose it and let yourself be carried along the stitch length.

2. **Zigzag:** used in cases where you want the fabric to not fray or to reinforce the edges of the seams. The length is also adjustable in it.

3. **Buttonholes:** This sewing process can be done in 4 steps or in one. This will depend on the machine you are using. However, making buttonholes is fairly straightforward.

4. **Invisible hem: This** is a discreet stitch that is not noticeable. For this you must use a color of thread that resembles

the tone of the fabric. It is also a fairly easy stitch to learn.

Choose the length

If you have already chosen the type of stitch to use, it is time to **select** the stitch **length**. I recommend not choosing one that is not so long or short. When choosing the voltage, number 4 is generally selected.

Place the fabric

Place the fabric on the metal base. There you will find three stripes that **will guide you** during the stitch so that it does not twist while sewing. Some people are guided by the distance between the presser foot (the piece that goes down while sewing) and the edge of the fabric.

Once the fabric is attached to the presser foot, you can start sewing. To do this you must step on the pedal and make a finish of ½ cm at the end.

Guide to the fabric

Once you start, it's just a matter of **guiding the fabric** straight as the machine does the stitches. During this process it is important not to stop the fabric or throw it away while the machine is in motion.

If you come across a corner, make sure the needle is still nailed to the fabric. Then, raise your presser foot slightly and turn in the direction you need.

Check the work

When you have finished making your first stitches, the last step is to **take a look** to see how you have left.

It is very normal to have irregular stitches at first, or it is important to know where you failed and push yourself to improve. Remember that, it is about pedaling while you find the correct speed. Little by little your work will become more impeccable and beautiful. Do not hesitate!

Recommendations

If you are thinking of buying a sewing machine to **put into practice what you have learned**, the first thing you should do is inform yourself. To do this, investigate its characteristics, accessories and cost-quality ratio. This way you will choose the one that best suits your needs and budget.

Once you understand the **logic of how** the sewing machine works, everything will be easier. However, you can only do this by practicing over and over again.

Start with **simple projects** and straight stitches, so you can incorporate more and more new stitches and new techniques.

Don't forget to maintain your sewing machine to make sure it's always working perfectly.

Take care of your posture. Remember that poor posture can affect your health. To do this you must adjust the chair appropriately, use your hair while sewing and choose a bright place.

Pattern Selection on Scraps of Fabric

Sew straight

Have you already tried? When you start, it's not so easy to sew straight!

Sew right angle or broken line

Nor is it easy to sew a right angle or a broken line. But with a little explanation, it rolls on its own:

1. Right angle

2. Broken line

Sew rounding

To sew curves, nothing too complicated, you just have to be regular. To do this, you just need to go slowly and support your fabric well.

Sew a seam

Ohhh, don't believe, it will happen to you so often at the beginning that a little method to do this CLEANLY and CALMLY will not be useless.

Sew an applique

Ahhh! If you are there, it is because you have already advanced a little! You know how to sew straight, you have integrated the fact of sewing on the wrong side then turn your work over on the right side, and now you want to decorate your project.

Sew a buttonhole

There are sewing machines that do it all by themselves, and others that ask their master (sse) to be guided ... Whatever happens, at first it is scary! You have to try yourself on a scrap of fabric to be sure, but don't worry, it's very simple.

Apply pressure

Here we have taken the example with resin pressures (kam pressure). All you need is a pressure clamp adapted to the size of your pressure, and presto!

Make a transfer on fabric

An iron, a special fabric transfer paper (light fabric or dark fabric, you have the choice), a fabric, a basic inkjet printer and a nice image? You have it all!

Overcast

Here it is a question of sewing in a zigzag stitch the seam allowances, which will be invisible from the outside. You may think that it is useless if we do not see them? If you do not do this, the margins left raw may fray as you go (washing, wear against your skin or another fabric) and this could ultimately undo your good work! Don't you want that?

How to Maintain Sewing Machine

Sewing is one of the oldest trades, as well as the tools and implements for its implementation. Having a sewing machine in perfect condition is essential for your professional and personal jobs. Whether you are a professional or hobbyist, you need to know **how to maintain your sewing machine.**

A sewing machine is made up of moving parts, and in many occasions, susceptible to wear. Therefore, it is necessary to give priority to the maintenance of all its parts.

Stay with us until the end of the reading so you can see how to do it.

Importance of maintenance on sewing machines

Planning the timely maintenance of your sewing machine is vital if you are consistent in making. Even more so if you have a professional sewing machine, it works continuously for several hours a day.

Let's see **why it is important to keep your** sewing machine in optimal conditions.

Economy: Failure to perform proper and timely maintenance on your sewing machine will shorten its life. This will result in you having to replace it with a new one, which will affect your budget.

Performance: If you are in high demand for clothing and creations, you will not want your machine to break down. An unexpected failure will delay the fulfillment of your commitments, affecting your productivity and performance. This can be avoided with adequate maintenance.

Efficacy: If you neglect a sewing kit you will end up compromising its effectiveness. Its stitches, edges, and different functions can be diminished.

Availability: By executing a scheduled maintenance to your sewing equipment, you will have assured their availability. This will allow you to establish a precise work and delivery schedule for your orders.

Procedure of Sewing Machine Maintenance

Servicing your sewing machine is a simple task but requires precision. Let's see the steps to perform proper and effective maintenance are:

Removing dust

Dust **is one of the biggest causes of jams** and breakdowns in sewing machines of any model. That is why the first thing that we must remove to a greater extent is the dust.

For this we must have a brush and a soft bristle brush.

On many occasions, the dust accumulates and mixes with oil residues, forming lint layers that are difficult to remove. So we must have patience, perseverance and time available to remove all this dirt.

Some important parts from **where we must remove the dust are:**

- The needle holder.

- Reel holder

- The bobbin case

- Presser foot

- The inside of the bobbin case

In addition, all the parts that we can access, and where we notice dust, **must be well cleaned.**

The inner part

Not only external parts require in-depth maintenance. Also the inside of the sewing machine requires special treatment to guarantee its operation.

To do this **we must dismantle the presser foot** and the shuttle, to reach inaccessible corners.

If your machine uses a metal coil, you must disassemble it and dust it off. You should also remove the coil and check that it does not have dust or other harmful residues.

Greased

Once you have made sure that there is no dust inside the most important parts of the machine, you will proceed to greasing. Greasing your sewing machine will allow the most important moving parts to run smoothly.

You should know that you cannot apply oil to all the pieces that come to mind. In fact, the main piece to be oiled is **the bobbin case.**

You can also put oil on **the shuttle**, and on the needle bars. This will be enough to guarantee good moving parts mechanics.

It is not necessary to put a large amount of oil on the parts previously described. **With one drop in each piece it will be more than enough.**

Assemble and test

When you finish cleaning and oiling your sewing machine, it is recommended to try it immediately. This ensures that all parts have been placed in place and correctly.

It also serves to feel the difference in performance and that you can compare how it worked without proper maintenance, and **how it works after maintenance.**

In the following you can see how to maintain your sewing machine at home, quickly and easily.

Accessories required for Maintenance

As you have noticed, the maintenance of sewing machines is relatively simple. However, the effectiveness can be diminished if you do not use the correct materials and products. Let's see a list of the recommended products and accessories for this process:

Nylon Cleaning Brush Set

For a deep and effective cleaning it is necessary to use brushes with tiny and flexible bristles. That is why we recommend the use of the ZOEON brush set.

They are 10 brushes of 21 centimeters long, but with different styles on the tips.

It is ideal for reaching the most difficult to reach places on sewing machines. In addition, it can be used to clean other appliances with similar characteristics.

They are 10 brushes of 21 centimeters long, but with different styles on the tips.

It is ideal for reaching the most difficult to reach places on sewing machines. In addition, it can be used to clean other appliances with similar characteristics.

5pcs Double Pointed Sewing Machine Brushes

This brush incorporates a double pointed structure in its design. This allows cleaning with different shades of firmness.

The pack is made up of 5 brushes with the same characteristic. When one of the brushes deteriorates, you will have the substitute immediately.

Sewing machine oil, 100 ml

Another essential product for the maintenance of sewing machines is oil. This allows the lubrication of the moving parts, lengthening the useful life of the machine components.

This time we recommend using Alfa sewing machine oil. **Its 100 ml presentation is ideal for easy transport and use.**

This oil provides a protective coating to sewing machine parts that prevents corrosion and dust from damaging components.

The cap is designed to easily add oil at key locations on the sewing machine.

5 liter sewing machine oil

If you own a large company with many sewing machines, you will likely require a **large amount of oil**. For these cases, we recommend 5-liter sewing machine oil.

It is an oil designed for the maintenance of domestic machines, and also for industrial models. It is resistant to high temperatures, forming a durable and effective film.

Sewing Mannequins

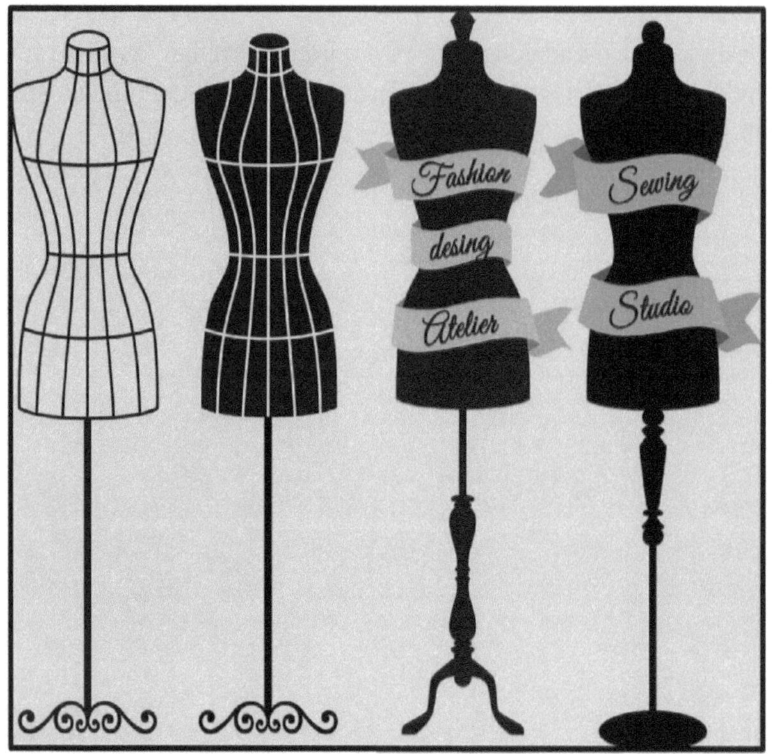

A **sewing mannequin** is a human-shaped figure that can generally be made of cardboard, plastic or wood. It is a product widely used by fashion designers, thanks to its many uses.

Sewing mannequins are used to display or display clothing. For this reason, today it is common to find them inside women's and men's clothing stores. Well, they **serve as visual appeal to channel more sales**.

Also, for dressmakers or fashion designers, an **adjustable mannequin** allows you to try on and fix items of clothing being made. So they can create new patterns or new garments with minimal margin for error.

The **mannequins sewing,** are highly recommended tools for making any outfit. Thanks to these, you can check how the garment looks, allowing you to detect inequalities and errors.

The mannequin can be used to test clothing, fit it and display it in your store. However, choosing a mannequin well, sometimes presents certain challenges. Especially if you do not know about its characteristics.

Types of Mannequins

Now I want you to know the different **types of mannequins that the market shows**. If you analyze them all in detail, it will surely be easier for you to identify which one you really need to carry with you.

- **Fixed or one size fits all**

The fixed mannequins or one-size-fits-all models are one-size-fits-all that do not allow for modification of their structure. Currently, they are often **used by sewing houses** and are preferred by many because they have affordable costs. In addition, they are made of different materials and with different finishes.

- **Adjustable or multi-size**

An adjustable, adjustable or multi-size mannequin is characterized by having mechanisms that allow it to adjust to different measurements. In this way, you can work with thin clients or thick build.

- **Display dress**

With **Display Dress mannequins** you will be guaranteed to make pieces with more freedom. Well, these are distinguished by presenting a complete structure similar to the human body. Thus, you will make better prom dresses, no matter how long they are.

- **Professional dress mannequin**

Professional dress mannequins are **three-dimensional models that allow**

garments that are being made to be worn. Some of these are designed with the body measurements of specific people. In addition, they are special for fashion designers with long experience.

- **Forked**

Forked mannequins have **removable legs and arms**. Thanks to this fantastic feature, expert tailors, fashion students or designers can make patterns and arrange garments with greater precision, as if the client were in front of them.

Tips for choosing the best sewing mannequin

I know you want to **buy the perfect mannequin**. Therefore, below I want to offer you some tips that will help you make the right decision when making your purchase. Come on!

What are you going to need it for?

Before making the purchase, it is pertinent that you know exactly **what use you will give the mannequin**. In this way, you will avoid purchasing a product with the opposite characteristics to your needs.

Remember that some **sewing mannequins** are adjustable and allow you to work more freely. Although if you want to create clothes for yourself, perhaps a fixed model can work just as well for you.

Find a balanced and homogeneous one

Buying an **adjustable sewing mannequin** may be the alternative you were looking for to replace your old mannequins. These are integral and you can use them to make original garments, as store displays or to locate them as striking decorations.

The most important thing is to acquire a model that allows you to make the most of it. In this way, you will feel very **satisfied with your investment**.

That the material and its base are of good quality.

As you will know the manufacturing materials, they are the guarantee of their quality, resistance and durability. Therefore, this is a feature that you cannot ignore when you go to make your purchase.

The best sewing mannequins are made of **foam covered by nylon fabric**. Also, try to select a model with the base made of oak or metal. These materials will not disappoint you!

It has a washable cover and can be removed

Aesthetics are important when we work with fashion design. For this reason, a characteristic that cannot be missing in your new mannequin is that it has a **removable and washable cover**. In this way, you can easily wash it every time it gets dirty due to daily use until it looks like new.

That allows to fix pins

All the models you found in this post are made **of good quality foam**. Therefore, they allow to fix pins easily and without running the risk that their structure deteriorates.

This feature is very important, since it will allow you to fix the ready-made garments whenever you want.

Versatility

It is important to acquire a mannequin that offers you great versatility when working. For example, there are **adjustable mannequins in different sizes**. Some are so complete that you can design complex garments such as ball gowns, pants, and blouses or shirts.

By gender

You can find **female, male** and even children's **mannequins**. The choice will depend on the pieces you are going to make. However, at this point it is important to consider the above tips.

Finally, if you wonder **where to buy sewing mannequins?** Remember that on the internet you have a wide range of options. You just have to look for a website that guarantees you better benefits, offers and discounts.

Tips to Buy Sewing Machine Furniture

To purchase a table that meets your particular needs, you must be aware of certain factors. Not all tables have the same characteristics. In this sense, we bring you some **tips that will help you** buy the best furniture for sewing machines.

- **Surface:** Find a table with the surface you would like to have. A wide table will make your work easier.

- **Machine:** The tables are generally designed for machines of general dimensions. It would be nice if you verified that your machine is perfectly compatible with the table.

- **Space:** Choose a table whose dimensions match the space you have. If you don't have that much space, many of these tables have a folding design that takes up little space when they are no longer in use.

- **Comfort:** Always look for a piece of furniture that offers you great comfort when working. If you can try it before buying it would be ideal.

- **Aesthetics:** It is not unnecessary to appreciate the style, color, material, etc. After all, it will be part of your home's furniture, and you want it to match it. Colors such as white, black or wood could easily adapt to any space.

- **Storage:** It is ideal that the furniture has compartments in which you can store your implements and sewing materials.

How to Sew Basic Clothing Items

Plain Shirt

It took me a while to make my first shirt after a few attempts with the wrong patterns. But I finally got there and I am very proud of the result even if, with the shirt barely finished. I simply unstitched one of my old shirt and I used it as a pattern, with some corrections of course.

Using an existing item of clothing that we like and that looks good on us is a good way to get clothes that are the right size.

I chose a very beautiful plaid fabric, among the fabrics for men's shirts. Personally, I appreciate man fabrics much more than simple plain cottons in which we generally make blouses for women.

Here are the technical points that I worked on making this shirt:

- Wrist

- The neck

- Buttonholes and buttons

Wrist fitting

For mounting the wrist, again you will find the tutorial on the Poitiers Academy website. I still give you four of my little tips that will be useful if like me you make the choice to make your wrist with two pieces:

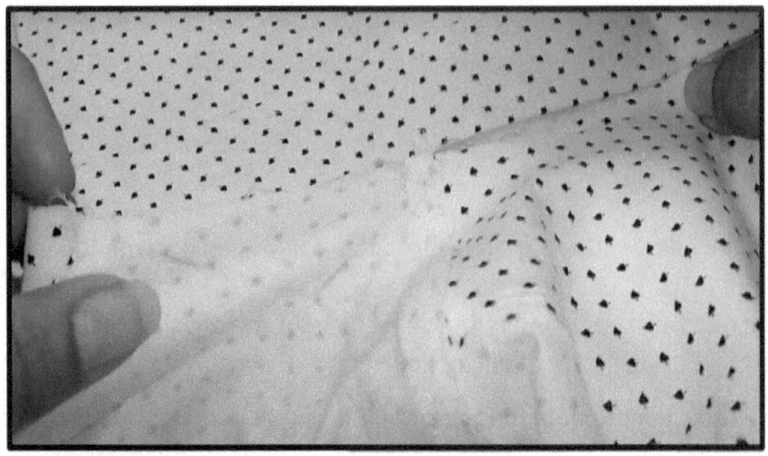

For the fusible, I advise you to hollow out the corners before applying it. Forming the wedge will be easier and you will have less thickness when you topstitch.

When you join the two sides of the wrist, you can slip a piece of wire to help you form the corner. When you reach the end of your side, slide the thread and make a stitch by turning the hand wheel to wedge the thread in the seam. Turn your fabric to sew the other side, lift the presser foot and slide the thread between the two fabrics then continue your sewing. When turning your wrist to form the corners, you will just have to pull on the thread, after obviously having hollowed out the corners and opened the seams

When overstitching the wrists, you can slip a thread in the two corners to help your machine pass this thickness by pulling (gently) on the thread

When I overstitch, I no longer make a breakpoint because it makes a seam a little thick and unsightly. I simply put the threads on the wrong side and make a knot.

The neck

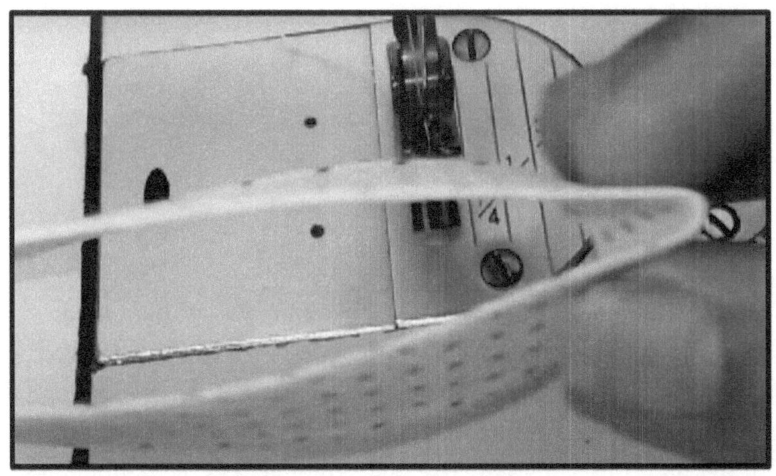

To make my collar, I used the thread technique mentioned above to make beautiful angles and, above all, when you iron the amount of the collar once turned, make sure to roll the seam underneath so that it is invisible once the collar is fitted.

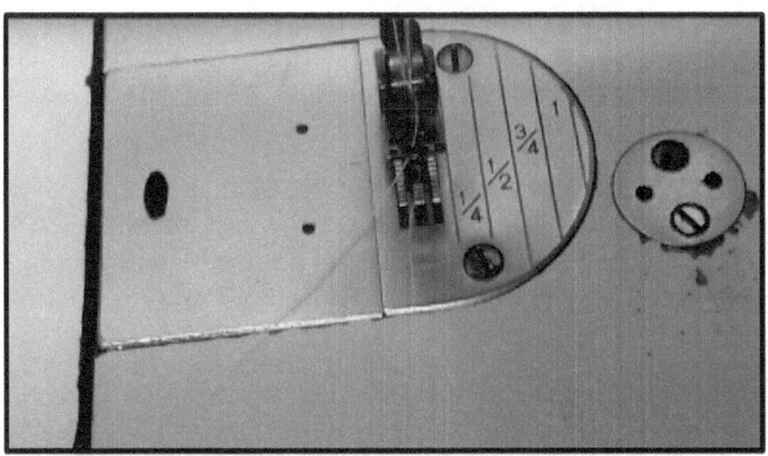

Making the buttonholes is a delicate step. First of all, care must be taken to put them on the right side. For women, the buttonholes are on the right and the buttons on the left.

To place the buttons, here are the rules to follow:

- Place a button on the chest line

- Place a button on the waist line

- Place the first button 5 or 6 cm from the neck

I advise you to take your time and give it a try. Making the buttonholes is a delicate step. It is the execution of the finishes that makes the quality of the garment. Once the location of the buttonholes is chosen, I advise you to make several tests for the size of the buttonholes with the buttons you have chosen. For my part, I love my new machine which makes the buttonholes all by itself!

For the buttons, as I do not have the adequate element to sew them with my machine, I have sewn them by hand, which is a good training for the CAP.

A difficulty was added for me: the reasons. Choosing a patterned fabric requires making connections: here the waist line and the shoulders. Note that for tiles, the smaller they are, the more difficult it is. I experimented with it by making two plaid shirts, the first before large tiles, the second with smaller tiles.

In addition, I made the choice not to overlock my seams but to make closed seams: for the shoulders, hemmed seams and for the sides and sleeves, false seams. I find that these finishes have a better effect and the shirt being a garment close to the body, the seams will be damaged less than if I had overlocked them.

Sewing a shirt is good training for CAP. This allows you to perform some techniques that you must know mastery for the exam. I hope I made you want to do it, even if you don't pass the CAP. The whole thing is to get started!

Basic Pajama Pants

If you are starting in the world of sewing, don't worry: making your own pants is not excessively complicated. Of course, before starting it is best that you inform yourself well about the steps you must follow.

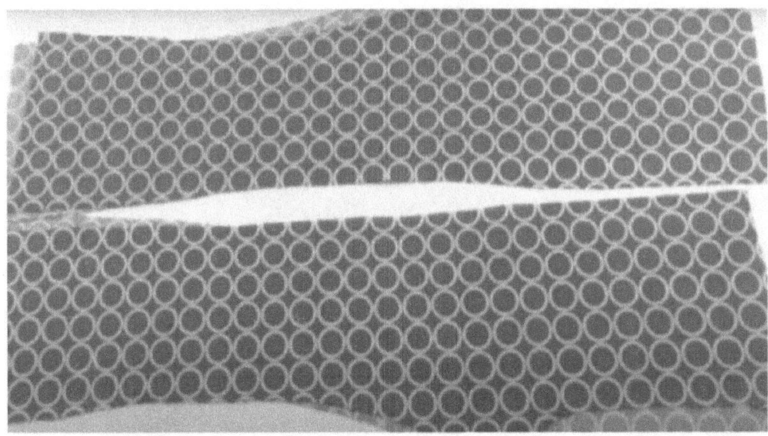

Choose the fabric of the pants

In order for you to move once you have it on, the fabric of the pants should be light, pleasant and solid. If you are starting, we advise you to use a cotton fabric, which will be easy to sew and manipulate.

Avoid fabrics that are difficult to work with, such as knitting, which is stretchy, or silk, which slips. Adapt the choice of fabric to the type of pants you want (satin, taffeta, to wear; denim, linen, etc., for a more informal Look.

Choosing a pant pattern

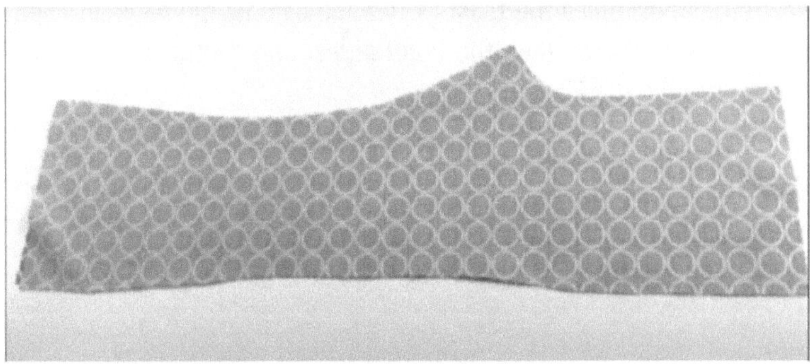

We recommend that you look for a pattern to make your own pants. The best thing is that you choose one that they have already tried, or that you start by making a first test pants with a fabric that does not cost much. The simplest pants are those with an elastic waist.

For the rest, the pattern should be more precise. The same goes for the U-shaped seam used between the legs - the pattern should serve as an accurate guide, without risking disappointing results.

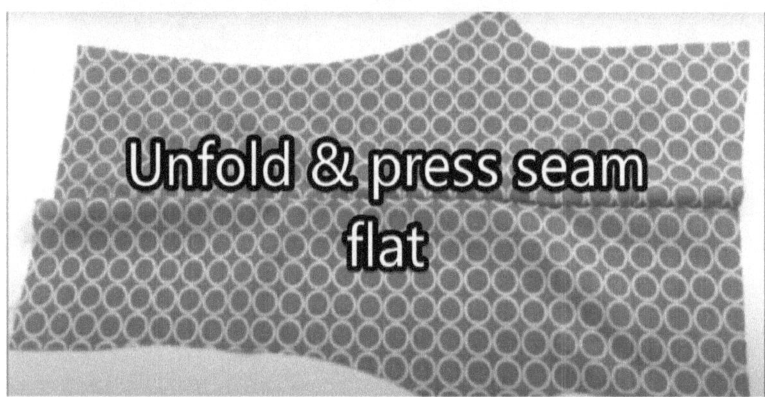

Put the pant legs together

Depending on the pattern you choose, you must put together the different pieces that make up the pants legs in one way or another. You must puncture the pieces and join the pieces of fabric that make up the front part of a leg and then the back part.

If your pants have pockets, remember to sew them before joining the legs. Once sewn together, place the front of one leg against the back and start to puncture the outer sides and then the inner sides, one centimeter from the edge and using a straight stitch.

Sew the union of the legs

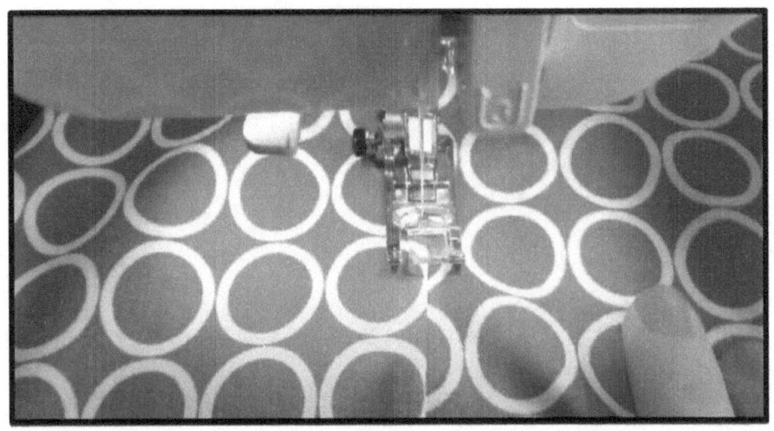

The union of the legs is one of the most delicate parts in the manufacture of pants, but with a good pattern and a little patience, you will achieve it without any problem. Lay the two legs side by side, crotch to crotch joint and waist to waist. Next, use pins to mark the seam and stitch a centimeter from the edge, with a straight stitch.

Give it the final touch

Once you have successfully completed these big steps, all you have to do is finish the pants: waist, hem, buttons, zipper or buttons on the fly part ... You decide the final touch!

Simple Cape

I unfolded my cape, measured, drawn to produce the pattern (front, back and sleeve):

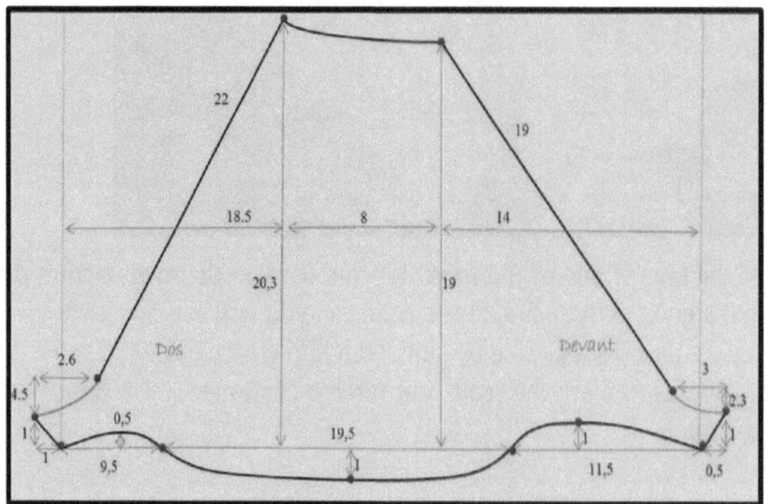

Here, me, I did my share of the work, it's up to you for the rest ...

But no, I'm not going to leave you like that ... some little extra tips (and with my approximate knowledge in sewing , you will have to hang on!):

- to reproduce the pattern, you have to position the pink dots thanks to the measures mentioned then link them
- add 1 cm of margins everywhere
- assemble front and back in the fabric
- the same with the lining
- assemble lining and fabric, right sides together, over the bottom and sides of the front (so do not touch the neckline or armholes)
- notch, turn the lining over
- assemble each sleeve
- assemble the sleeves to the rest of the work (they are not doubled): they are sewn right sides together with the fabric (also taking the lining: I therefore took the seams on the overlock foot of my machine, to that it is cleaner, maybe there is a way to do better)

- for the finishes of the sleeves: I made 3 small flat folds on the top and put an internal bias (that too, it must have a name, but I don't know: p)
- for the neckline: I just put a strip 6 cm wide (8 cm if we add the margins), folded in 2.
- all that remains is to sew the buttonholes and buttons ...

Red Carpet Dress in 20 Minutes

1. Imperative: Choose a heavy jersey that falls well, does not crumple, and with a little elastane is even better. The advantage in addition to the wonderful fall is that there is no need to hem!

2. Cut a square of 140 cm by 140 cm (applying yourself since the edges remain bare!) Allow more height for the large ones (I am 1.66m!)

3. Fold the fabric in half crosswise and 60 cm from the top, sew a 28 cm seam to join the two edges (the start should fall roughly at navel level). The bottom remains open.

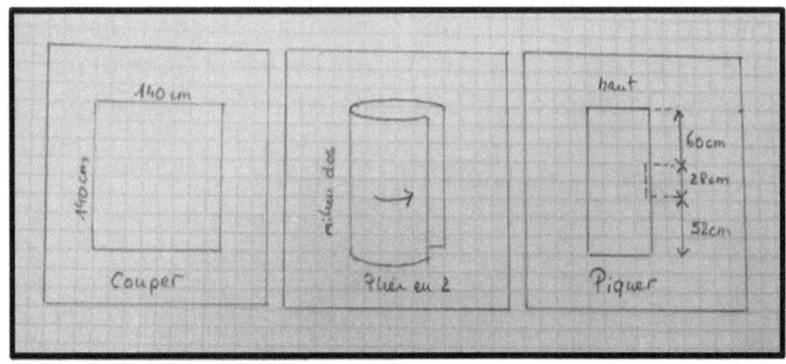

4. Turn right side, put on the dress by positioning the seam in front, grab the two free sides from the top, pull them to adjust the back, then cross them twice just above the chest and tie them behind the neck like a pareo!

5. Adjust the hem if necessary.

6. Slip your new dress into the suitcase!

And the second idea, because I didn't stop there! A sarong dress to put on over the swimsuit, the cut is very simple but the result is stunning, the drape forms all by itself at the neckline and lower back.

Sarong Dress

1. Choose a light fabric with a fluid drape.

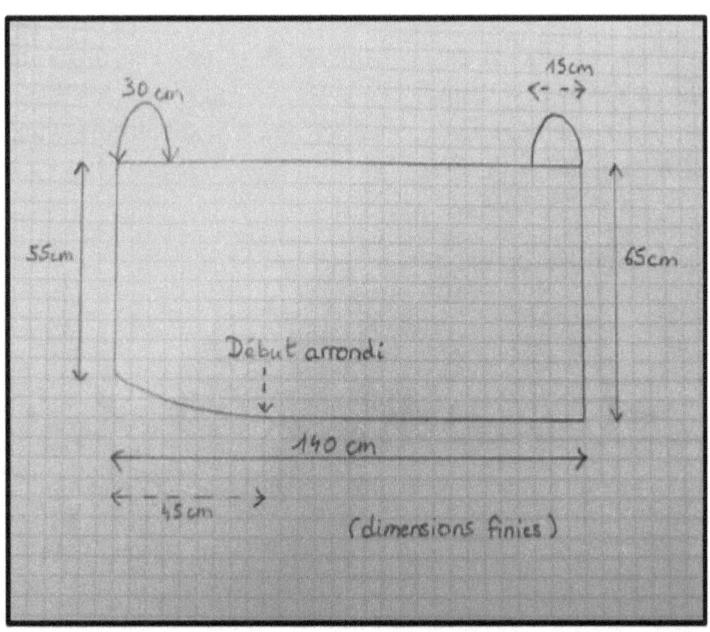

Cut a rectangle so as to obtain, after hemming, the dimensions of the diagram below:

1. Sew the side seams (for my fabric I used the MAC with a twin needle and cut the excess on the wrong side flush with the seam.

2. In the same way make the hem on the upper edge, then of the lower edge

3. The suspenders: In the scraps of fabric, form a tube 80 cm long by 1.5 wide (finished dimensions) To turn the tube after sewing, use a safety pin that you attach to one end, and make it slide inside, until it comes out, carrying the inverted fabric with it! Iron and cut in half.

4. Attach one end of each of the straps to one end of the upper edge (make two stitching: one near the edge and one over the stitching of the edge hem), then try and adjust before sewing the other end of the suspender.

5. Slip your new dress into the suitcase!